D1564546

Also by Frederick Seidel

THE COSMOS POEMS

GOING FAST

MY TOKYO

THESE DAYS

POEMS, 1959–1979

SUNRISE

FINAL SOLUTIONS

LIFE ON EARTH

LIFE ON EARTH

Frederick Seidel

FARRAR, STRAUS AND GIROUX

NEW YORK

Farrar, Straus and Giroux

19 Union Square West, New York 10003

Distributed in Canada by Douglas & McIntyre Ltd.

Printed in the United States of America

First edition, 2001

Library of Congress Cataloging-in-Publication Data

Seidel, Frederick, 1936–

Life on earth / Frederick Seidel.— 1st ed.

p.   cm.

ISBN 0-374-18685-5 (alk. paper)

I. Title

PS3569.E5 L54 2001

811'.54—dc21

00-045612

Designed by Peter A. Andersen

To my friend

PIERRE LEVAL

CONTENTS

LIFE ON EARTH

BALI

Is there intelligent life in the universe?
No glass
In the windows of the bus
In from the airport, only air and perfume.

Every porch in the darkness was lighted
With twinkling oil lamps
And there was music
At 2 a.m., the gamelan.

I hear the cosmos
And smell the Asian flowers
And there were candles
Mental as wind chimes in the soft night.

Translucency the flames showed through,
The heavy makeup the little dancers wore,
The scented sudden and the nubile slow
Lava flow of the temple troupe performing for the hotel guests.

Her middle finger touches her thumb in the *vitarkamudra,*
While her heavily made-up eyes shift wildly,
Facial contortions silently acting out the drama,
And the thin neck yin-yangs back and forth to the music.

Announcing the gods,
The room jerked and the shower curtain swayed.
All the water in the swimming pool
Trampolined out, and in the mountains hundreds died.

The generals wanted to replace Sukarno.
Because of his syphilis he was losing touch
With the Communist threat and getting rather crazy.
So they slaughtered the Communists and the rich Chinese.

Gentle Balinese murdered gentle Balinese,
And, in the usual pogrom, killed
The smart hardworking Chinese,
Merchants to the poor, Jews in paradise.

FRENCH POLYNESIA

Drinking and incest and endless ease
Is paradise and child abuse
And battered wives.
There are no other jobs.

Everything else is either
Food or bulimia.
The melon drips with this.
It opens and hisses happiness.

A riderless horse sticks out,
Pink as an earthworm, standing on the beach.
Fish, fish, fish,
I feel fishish.

I develop
When I get below my depth.
I splinter into jewels, Cadillac-finned balls,
Chromed mercury no one can grab.

I care below the surface.
Veils in
Colors I haven't seen in fifty years nibble
Coral.

Easter Sunday in Papeete.
Launched and dined at L'Acajou.
The Polynesians set off for outer space
In order to be born, steering by the stars.

Specialists in the canoes chant
The navigation vectors.
Across the universe,
A thousand candles are lighted

In the spaceships and the light roars
And the choir soars. A profusion
Of fruit and flowers in tubs being offered
Forms foam and stars.

III

THE OPPOSITE OF
A DARK DUNGEON

Three hundred steps down
From the top
Pilgrims are
Looking up.

The temple is above
In a cave.
The stairs to it start next
To the standard frantic street.

Monkeys beg on
The stairs
All the way
Up to the entrance.

Vendors sell treats
To the pilgrims to feed to them.
Some people are afraid of monkeys
Because they think they might get bitten.

When you finally reach the top, somewhat
Out of breath, you enter
The heavy cold darkness
And buy a ticket.

The twenty-foot gilded figures recline.
There are trinkets you can buy to lay at their smiling feet.
They use up the universe with their size.
Their energy is balm and complete.

Everything in the cosmos
Is in the cave, including the monkeys
Outside. Everything is
The opposite of a dark dungeon. And so

A messenger from light arrived.
Of course they never know that they're a messenger.
Don't know they carry a message.
And then they stay a while and then they leave.

STAR BRIGHT

The story goes one day
A messenger from light arrived.
Of course they never know that they're a messenger.
Don't know they carry a message.

The submarine stayed just
Below the surface with its engines off near the shore observing.
One day the world took off its shoes and disappeared
Inside the central mosque

And never came back out. Outside the periscope the rain
Had stopped, the fires on shore were
Out. Outside the mosque
The vast empty plaza was the city's outdoor market till

The satellite observed the changing
Colors of the planet
And reported to the submarine that
No one was alive.

A messenger from light arrived.
Of course they never know that they're a messenger.
Don't know they carry a message.
And then they stay a while and then they leave.

Arrived, was ushered in,
Got in a waiting car and drove away.
Was ushered in,
Kowtowed to the Sacred Presence the required ten times

And backed away from the Sacred Presence blind,
And turned back into light.
Good night,
Blind light.

Far star, star bright.
And though they never know that they're a messenger,
Never know they carry a message,
At least they stay a while before they leave.

V

GOODNESS

In paradise on earth each angel has to work.
Jean-Louis de Gourcuff and his wife spend hours
Spreading new gravel in the courtyard and the drive.
The château swan keeps approaching its friend Jean-Louis to help.

Monsieur le Comte et Madame la Comtesse
Have faith, give hope, show charity.
This is the Château of Fontenay.
And this is the Gourcuffs' ancient yellow lab, Ralph.

It's de rigueur for French aristocrats to name their dogs in English.
Something about happiness is expressed
By the swan's leaving the safety of its pond,
Given the number of English names around.

Ralph smiles and says *woof* and the swan smiles and says *hiss*
In a sort of Christian bliss.
What is more Christian than this?
You have entered the kingdom of the kind.

Old Count de Gourcuff lives in another wing, the father,
Tall big-boned splendor of an English gentleman, but French.
His small wife is even more grand and more France.
One has a whisky with him in the library.

Something about goodness is being expressed
At a neighbor's château nearby.
In the marble reception hall, ghosts are drinking champagne.
The host will be shot right afterward by the Nazis for something.

Blind Ralph barks at the hissing swan he waddles behind and adores.
It is left to the childlike to lead the sick and the poor.
Jean-Louis de Gourcuff, the saintly mayor of Fontenay,
Dons his sash of office, white, blue, and red.

Dominique de Gourcuff makes regular
Pilgrimages with the infirm, to refresh her heart, to Lourdes.
Dinosaurs on their way to being birds
Are the angels down here in heaven.

JOAN OF ARC

Even her friends don't like her.
Tears roll out of
Her tear ducts,
Boulders meant to crush.

She feels
Her own emptiness but oddly
It feels like love
When you have no insight at all

Except that you are good.
The tears crush even
That thought out and she is left happily
Undressed with her stupidity.

Nobody wants her
On their side in games at school
So the retard
Is wired to explode.

She smokes, gets drunk,
Gets caught, gets thrown out
As the ringleader when she was not since
She has no followers, this most innocent

Who is completely
Emptiness,
Who is a thrill no one wants and
Whom the cowed will kill.

The "Goddamns" (as the invading English are
Called) get in her France.
It made the Maid of Orleans a man and God
Hears her crewcut rapture screaming at the stake in pants.

For God's sake, the food is burning
On the stove!
You are the only one in the world.
You are my good girl.

DOCTOR LOVE

It was a treatment called
Doctor Love, after the main character.
One of the producers discovered
To our horror a real

Dr. Love who, eerily, by
Pure coincidence, was also a woman
Oncologist trying to identify the gene that causes
Breast cancer. My

Fiction trampolined
Herself right off the treatment page,
Landing not on a movie set or a screen at the multiplex,
But at a teaching hospital in Los Angeles directing

Her lab. If you could identify the gene
That turns the cancer on,
Then maybe you could find a way to turn it off—
And make somebody rich.

She found a gene.
The villain needed to learn which.
He sets the innocent doctor up to
Commit a murder. The story was in such bad taste.

It never made sense.
I was doing rounds in a long white coat
To write the screenplay—playing doctor, doctor love.
Till death us do part, Dr. Catharine Hart,

I will remember you
On the street kissing me hello.
The cherry blossom petals blow—
White coats on rounds

In a soft East River breeze—like glowing fireflies of snow.
Dear Hart, it is spring.
Cutting a person open
Is possible without pain.

FEVER

Your pillow is pouring
You like a waterfall
You sleep through
In the middle of.

You shiver sweat
In the middle of
The rain forest chattering in
Darkness at midday.

You like heat because
It makes a reptile warm.
On the raft with you
Is your life.

You have everything
You have.
The crocodiles choo-chooing around
And around are the snouts

Of your ancestors
Which split and jaggedly yawn
Because it is time to
Read aloud

The story
Of the African slaves walking on water
In chains all the way to the United States
In 1776.

Two hundred–plus years later,
Islam overthrows the Shah.
No Menstruation Women Allow,
A temple sign had said on Bali.

The temple monkeys had not been friendly.
The president of the rubber-stamp Iranian senate,
Sharif-Imami, the loathed Shah
Loved. The fever breaks.

BLOOD

The yellow sunlight with
The milky moonlight makes
An egg without cholesterol
And I will live.

O tree of brains
And sound of leaves.
The day is green.
And now I pray.

I thank the cotton
For the shirt.
I thank the glass that holds me
In, that I see through into out there.

I'm driving to the car wash
And the dogs are getting haircuts
And the motorcycles drive by
And I ask for mine,

My body in your hands
To live.
The bay is blue
To me means that.

The saline breeze says that
The soft is firm enough today
To hold the water up
With gulls on top that won't

Sink in.
I don't know when.
I don't know how.
I don't know I.

I tell the cardiologist that
I'm in love.
The needle draws the champagne
Into crystal flutes the lab will love.

HOLLY ANDERSEN

I describe you.
I have a chart to.
I hold your
Heart. I feel.

The motor
Of your life
Is not diseased or weak
Or real until

I stress it from the
Outside, how
You test anyone before you
Find them true.

Totally in
Your power,
The stethoscope
Puts its taproot to your chest, and flowers.

The miles of
Treadmill agnostically
Takes core samples.
The bolus which jump-starts us back to life is love.

The light leaps and is living
On the screen
As the mine-detector mechanism
Looks for mines.

Take a deep breath.
You stopped smoking cigarettes.
Breathe out through your mouth.
How many years ago.

We are made of years
That keep on living.
We are made of tears
That as your doctor I can't cry.

AT NEW YORK HOSPITAL

I enter the center.
I open the book of there.
I leave my clothes in a locker.
I gown myself and scrub in.

Anything is possible that I do.
Cutting a person open
Is possible without pain. An entourage rolls
In a murderous head of state with beautiful big breasts—

Who is already under and extremely nude
On the gurney. Her sheet has slipped off.
Her perfect head has been shaved
Bald. And now a target area

On the top of the skull will
Be painted magenta. Her body is re-wrapped.
Her face gets sealed off. Her crimes against humanity
Will be lasered.

I am a Confederate scout, silence in the forest.
The all eyes and stillness
Of a bird watcher has stumbled on
A Yankee soldier asleep.

The dentist's drill drills a hole and
The drill slips and whines out of control,
But no matter. The electric saw cuts
Out a skullcap of bone.

The helicopter descends from Olympus to within an
Inch of touching down
On the wrinkled surface, when a tool falls incredibly
To the floor and I pick it up and am thanked.

The anesthesiologist for my benefit joyously
Declaims Gerard Manley Hopkins.
The surgeon recites a fervent favorite childhood hymn.
He slaps the monster tenderly to wake her up. Wake up, darling.

DRINKS AT THE CARLYLE

The pregnant woman stares out the spaceship window at space—
But is listening carefully.
The man is looking at the inward look on her face.
The man is answering her question while they leave the galaxy.

Why they are on this space voyage neither stranger quite knows.
There is something that
Someone watching them
Might feel almost shows,

But would not be able to say what.
She was describing the American child
She was, the athlete who played the violin,
Who grew up on Earth upstate.

He sees American thrust, the freckled ignition
Who vanished in a puff of smoke on stage—and the power and
Grandly pregnant happily married woman physician
There on stage when the smoke cleared. He looks at her left hand

And her bow hand. He sees the child lift the half-size violin
From its case, and take the bow,
And fit the violin to her shoulder and chin,
And begin to saw, sweetly, badly,

While she asks him what it is like to be him,
To be a space commander, revered.
He stares softly at her severed
Connection to him as she again looks inward

And very distantly smiles
While he tries to think what she is asking him and answer.
She is smartly dressed in black,
Blond midnight in the air-conditioned hot middle of summer.

She has smilingly said she is the only doctor in town on
Fridays in July, so she knows everything.
It is amazing what people actually do.
I am not possible to know.

CHIQUITA GREGORY

Sagaponack swings the Atlantic around its head
Like an athlete in the windup for the hammer throw.
It is a hurricane and the radio
Predicts a tornado will follow.

The air violently
Smells fresh like nowhere else,
And I am just assuming it is
You calling to everyone lunch is ready.

We are heads bowed
At our place cards. Zeus is saying grace
When the chairs begin to shake and lightning outside
Shazams you back to life, tsunami

Light as a feather, the feather of life,
Very long legs,
Very short shorts, a chef's apron in front, so that from
Behind . . . Goddess,

You have returned to earth in a mood and
In a storm, and I have no doubt that
Irreplaceable trees on Sagg Main are davening
Themselves to the ground. They

Rend their clothes and tear their hair out out
Of joy. Chiquita, how can anyone be so
Angry who has died? The whirling light in
The drive is the police, here

To urge the last holdouts in houses near the
Ocean to leave. To help us
Decide, they suavely ask for the name of next of kin.
The ocean bursts into towering flames of foam.

The lobsters in the pot are screaming
Inside the reddening roar.
Your aproned ghost keeps boiling more, keeps boiling more,
And turns to serve the gore.

TO START AT END

To start at End
And work back
To the mouth
Is the start—

Back to the black hole
That ate the meal,
Back from the universe
And the book

To the illiteracy
Of the much too
Compressed pre-universe
To release. So it was

The hands of fingers on
The keyboard bringing up on the screen
The something thirteen
Billion light-years back that happened,

The *Gentlemen, start your engines!*
That made it start,
Which is the mouth
Of the music.

The uncontrollable
Is about to happen—
A gash in the nothingness invisibly
Appears.

The uncontrollable is about
To happen—the strings (of String Theory)
Are trembling unseen ecstatically
Before they even are touched by the bow.

It all happened so fast.
The fall weather was vast.
At either end of space-time the armies massed.
Youth was past.

XV

WE HAVE IGNITION

Infinity was one of many
In a writhing pot of spaghetti.
One among many
Intestines of time.

The
Trembling the size and color
Of boiled lobster coral
Was trying

More violently than anything
Could and still live. The
Subatomic particles
Were

The truth. One of them became
The universe at once
While the others fled.
And one —

Not our universe —
Became something else.
Don't think about it
And you won't.

The landmass of the continental
United States compared to an open
Manhole
On the bitter boulevard where citizens buy crack

Is how much bigger the human brain is
Than the entire universe was at the start,
When it was the prickle
Before the zit.

Godspeed, John Glenn.
Fly safely high
In your seventy-seven-year-old
Head thirteen billion years old.

ETERNITY

A woman waits on a distant star she is traveling to.
She waits for herself to arrive.
But first she has to embark.
3, 2, 1 . . . ignition.

All systems are go for the facelift.
Her face lifts off into space.
She heads for the distant star
And the young woman waiting for her there.

A man who wanted to look better
But not younger is red
Swells of raw.
Later they will remove the staples.

Ten weeks later
They are younger.
They pull over
Their head a sock of skin.

One day the girl sees in the mirror a girl
Laughing so hard her face falls off in her hands.
You can see the inside of the face.
The front of her head is an amputee's smooth stump.

Her old woman's body is a bag of spotted slop.
The gentleman at least is doing fine.
His face peeks through the shower curtains
Of his previous face.

In the tomb air
Of the spacecraft they get more perfumed
As they painstakingly near
The hot banks of the Nile, so green and fertile.

Heart is safe in a dish of preservative.
Face is a box for the telemetry for the journey.
Perishable slaves caravan the monumental blocks of stone to the site.
The faceless likeness deafens the desert.

THE MASTER JEWELER
JOEL ROSENTHAL

What's Joel
Got to do but let the jewel
Hatch
The light and hook

It to the flesh
It will outlast
And point the staring
Woman at a mirror?

The stone alone was fireworks
But is Star Wars in his choker.
Of course Joel wears no jewelry himself but
Makes it for these reasons rhyme.

The staring woman is starving and
Eating her own face and
Stares with a raving smile
At her undying love.

The things they
Have to have
Are his
Designs on them.

The richest in the world stick out their necks
And hands and ears for JAR's gems—
Which they can ride through the eye of a needle
To heaven. His genius is his

Joy, is JAR, is
Agonized obsession, is death is double-parked
Outside the palace. Death is loading in the van
The women and camels of King Solomon it is repossessing.

Joel has designed a watch
In platinum.
This watch is the sequel
To anyone you have ever lost.

XVIII

IN SPITE OF EVERYTHING

I had a question about the universe
On my way to my evening class,
Stuck between stations on the No. 3 Express,
And it was this.

You don't know what you mean
And that's what I mean.
God is playing peekaboo,
Not There behind the hands.

Then peekaboo and you
See face-to-face and bam.
I'm getting old.
I hid and I revealed myself.

All the way down to the wharf
All the way down to the wharf
All the way down to the wharf
He-wolf and she-wolf went walking.

Shut up, darling! I'll do the talking.
All the way down to the wharf
All the way down to the wharf
The stalker was stalking.

The talker was talking.
You want to talk
Until I droop.
The river runs by

Under the broken pier.
All the great ocean liners left for France from here,
Whose passengers are
Now ghosts mostly. Loup and Louve howl

To Neptune from their heaving gale-force stateroom—
Walk through drought, walk through dew,
Keep walking down the avenue,
For richer for poorer, for better for worse, malgré tout.

XIX

SPRINGTIME

Sunset rolls out the red carpet
For Charlotte as she walks
To her appointment with life
In the awed soft-focus.

Charlotte sees the crimson trees
With her famous eyes.
Fat rises to the surface of the street in sunset flames.
The magnolias are vomiting brightness

In the mist. Spring in its mania refuses
To take its medication. It
Buys every newspaper left on the newsstand, then
Sobs in a café, sobs with laughter.

A car at a light rocks from side to side with the
Windows down, letting in red, letting out rhythm—
A pounding pulse of rap from the exophthalmic car radio.
She would give anything to be able to

Sleep in a shower of this fragrance.
She is talking on her fear
Phone to anyone in her mind. She is
Saying in a red city

I am alive at sunset.
Charlotte is beautiful but
Charlotte is so beautiful it is
Insolence.

A fan
Asks for her autograph outside a restaurant.
Horse carriages slowly carry
Honeymooners through a fog of love as thick as snow.

A slave to love
Kisses a real slave she bought to free.
The dominatrix is whipped by her slave—
Who has made a mistake on the new rug and wags.

XX

SUMMER

Kitsy and Bitsy and Frisky and Boo
Stream by, memories of moist
Moss—green morphine—
On each bank of a stream.

Fronds as delicate
As my feelings present
Those summers.
You could drink the water you swam

In, clear, cold, sweet, but August,
But August in St. Louis,
But August and the heat
That slows the green smell of the lawns

To tar, lyric
Of humidity
That thickens to a halt, but sweet, that swells
Up, that you escaped to dreams

From. In one,
Beauty and kindness combined
To walk across a room.
The daughter of Colonel Borders, Kitsy,

Means God has found a way, walks in through a door.
The universe begins at once.
The stars erupt a sky
They can be stars in, that they can be

Unicorns in a pen in.
The perfect knight in armor to slay the fiery dragon
Has sex with it instead.
I wake from the dream in the dark.

I barely see above
The steering wheel at twelve years old.
The park at night is warm.
The air is sweet and moist and cool.

XXI

FALL SNOWFALL

The book of nothingness begins
At birth.
The pages turn and there
Is far.

There is far from where
They start.
The pages turn into
The book.

And everything and everyone and
What is happening
Is blood in urine.
Ask the trees

The leaves leave.
They are left.
They remove their wigs.
They turn themselves in.

They stand there blank.
The now falls
On the fields white.
The smell of wood smoke stares and

The no falls,
Radios
Of blank now
On the fields.

A black crow shakes the no off.
Merrily we
Go around circling
The drain, life is but a dream.

The doctors in their white
No
Fall
On the fields.

XXII

CHRISTMAS

My Christmas is covered
With goosepimples in the cold.
Her arms are raised straight
Above her head.

She turns around slowly in nothing but a
Garter belt and stockings outdoors.
She has the powerful
Buttocks of a Percheron.

My beautiful with goosepimples
Climbs the ladder to the high diving board
In her high heels
And ideals.

The mirror of the swimming pool is looking up at her
Round breasts.
She bounces up and down
As if about to dive.

In her ideals, in her high heels,
The palm trees go up and down.
The mirror of the swimming pool is looking up at her
Bikini trim.

The heated swimming pool mirror is steaming
In the cold.
The Christmas tree is on.
A cigarette speedboat cuts the bay in two.

It rears up on its white wake.
Ay, Miami!
Ninety miles away
Is Mars.

The cigarette smokes fine cigars,
Rolls hundred dollar bills into straws.
My Christmas
Is in his arms.

XXIII

COSMOPOLITANS AT THE PARADISE

Cosmopolitans at the Paradise.
Heavenly Kelly's cosmopolitans make the sun rise.
They make the sun rise in my blood
Under the stars in my brow.

Tonight a perfect cosmopolitan sets sail for paradise.
Johnny's cosmopolitans start the countdown on the launch pad.
My Paradise is a diner. Nothing could be finer.
There was a lovely man in this town named Harry Diner.

Lighter than zero
Gravity, a rinse of lift, the cosmopolitan cocktail
They mix here at the Paradise is the best
In the United States—pink as a flamingo and life-announcing

As a leaping salmon. The space suit I will squeeze into arrives
In a martini glass,
Poured from a chilled silver shaker beaded with frost sweat.
Finally I go

Back to where the only place to go is far.
Ahab on the launch pad—I'm the roar
Wearing the wild blazer, black stripes and red,
And a yarmulke with a propeller on my missile head.

There she blows! Row harder, my hearties!—
My United Nations of liftoff!
I targeted the great white whale black hole.
On impact I burst into stars.

I am the Caliph of paradise,
Hip-deep in a waterbed of wives.
I am the Ducati of desire,
144.1 horsepower at the rear wheel.

Nights and days, black stripes and red,
I orbit Sag Harbor and the big blue ball.
I pursue Moby-Dick to the end of the book.
I raise the pink flamingos to my lips and drink.

XXIV

SEX

The woman in the boat you shiver with
The sky is coming through the window at.
We will see.
Keep rowing.

You have
An ocean all around.
You are rowing on bare ground.
The greasy grassless clay is dead calm.

You love your life.
You love the way you look.
You watch a woman posing for you.
How awful for you. There's no one there.

Inside the perfume bottle life is sweet.
The glass stopper above you is the stars.
You smell the flowers,
Some far-off shore.

The slaves are chained in rows rowing.
The motion back and forth
Is the same as making love.
You fuck infinity and that takes time.

It's a certain way of talking to arthritis
That isn't heart disease or trust.
You can't remember why
Your hands are bleeding back and forth.

The thing about a man is that—
Is what?
One hand reaches for the other.
The other has a knife in it to cut the head off.

The fish flops back and forth
In the bottom of the boat.
The woman pulls the boat along
By its painter that the king slash slave is rowing.

XXV

SONG

How small your part
Of the world is when
You are a girl.
The forests and deserts are full

Of the animals
We ride and eat
And the wind and the light
And the night,

But if you are
A girl you may
As well live in Boston
Or be a grain of white rice

Or be a fleck
Of mica in a sidewalk.
I wanted to have
A monocle and stick—

Put on my top hat,
And be a grain
Of radium,
And radiate a stadium with my act.

It's about holding
The wide-eyed bearded head of
Holofernes
Aloft. From the carrier deck

We climb to altitude
With an attitude, with
Our laser-guided bombs targeting
The white enormous whale.

We need the sperm oil to light
Our lamps, have to stop
The huge white life for whalebone stays to cage
Our corsets.

XXVI

THE SEAL

What did the vomit of a god
Smell like? Like no one else
And there were clouds of it
In the White House.

It was an impeachable
U.S. bald eagle
Because it was barking and sporting
In the moisture like a seal.

Tubby smooth
Energy tube of seal seeks tender veal
For the White House mess and in a zoo
It smells like that.

To be slick
And sleek and swim
And in yours have hers,
Her hand, her heart.

Once it was a god,
Now they toss it fish
And watch it leap
And make it beg.

They're looking
At TV and look
It doesn't look that bad.
The ones from outer space are landing now.

A seal went out to play
In the middle of an enormous bay
All the cities surrounded,
The size of the Dust Bowl, as brown,

And sang of a 21st century that was lyrical
About effluents and landfill,
And set the presidential seal
On doing something about race and ass.

XXVII

HER SONG

I am presenting
Myself to
You for the punishment
I preserve.

Sometimes you seem to
Understand I am
Banished.
I am the emptiness of

Bandages
That wrap
The mummy. My heart
I preserve in a dish—

It is a dog collar on all fours.
Inside is the
Eloquence
Emptied out.

Your hand
Starts to thunder,
Starts to rain much
Harder.

You raised your hand
To touch my cheek.
You saw my eyes
Go berserk.

It is the terror.
It asks you
To make it more.
Don't fall

In love
With me and I won't either.
Don't stop when
I say stop.

XXVIII

GREEN DRESS, 1999

You want
To change your name to be new
For the
Millennium so do.

The trumpet sounds
Your smile.
You soar just
Sitting still.

Flapping wings of a
Flamingo, clouds
Of my angina
Blossom darkly into dawn.

Sunset follows
While they play
The songs one wants
To hear. Your

Legs made of eleven
Kinds of heaven
Leap to
Where they want to go.

But I don't know
How long I have the
Future for.
In the jungle of

The body is the beating of the
Tom-tom.
Living dot com—
How many hits on your site?

If dance is what you do, the bar
Is where you go to
Work. If what you do is drink,
You also hit the heart.

XXIX

LETTER TO
THE EDITORS OF *VOGUE*

I'm seeing someone and
I really want to,
But I
Am stuck in glue.

I would go anywhere
To be near
The sky above
And smell the iodine

Wine of the port of Algiers,
Or for that matter the freezing
Nights on the dunes
Of the Sahara are blood

That you can drink till dawn
Under the terror of
Stars to
Make you blind.

I am drinking gasoline
To stay awake
In the midst of so much
Murder.

My daughter squeaks and squeaks
Like a mouse screaming in a trap,
Dangling from the cat who makes her come
When he does it to her.

Her killer goes out into
The streets to join his brothers
In the revolution
Who don't have jobs.

The *plastic* packed beautifully
Inside a tampons box that I carefully leave in the loo
At Café Oasis goes rigid and the
Unveiled meet God.

XXX

JAMES BALDWIN IN PARIS

The leopard attacks the trainer it
Loves, over and over, on every
Page, loves and devours the only one it allows to feed
It.

How lonely to be understood
And have to kill, how lovely.
It does make you want to starve. It makes an animal kill
All the caring-and-sharing in the cage.

Start with the trainer who keeps you alive
In another language,
The breasts of milk
That speak non-leopard. Slaughter them.

What lives below
The surface in a leopard will have to live above
In words. I go to sleep
And dream in meat and wake

In wonder,
And find the poems in
The milk
All over the page.

Lute strings of summer thunder, rats hurrying
Away, sunshine behind
Lightning on a shield of
Pain painting out happiness, equals life

That will have to be extinguished
To make way. The sound trucks getting out the vote
Drive the campaign song down every street.
Hitler is coming to Harlem.

Hitler is coming to Harlem! / There will be ethnic cleansing. /
A muddy river of Brown Shirts / Will march to the Blacks.
Happiness will start to deface
Pain on the planet.

XXXI

ST. LOUIS, MISSOURI

You wait forever till you can't wait any longer—
And then you're born.
Somebody is pointing something out.
You see what I'm saying, boy!

Can't find a single egg at his debutant
Easter egg hunt and has to be helped.
Jewish wears a little suit with a shirt with an Eton collar.
Blood cakes on the scratch on your little knee.

Excuse me a minute.
The angel is black as a crow.
The nurse comes back in the room.
It shakes the snow from its wings.

The waterfall hangs
Down panting in the humidity.
The roar at the top of the world
Is the icebergs melting in pain.

Don't play on the railroad tracks.
It is so hot.
The tracks click before you hear the train
Which the clicks mean is coming.

British consuls posted to St. Louis in those days
Before air conditioning had to receive extra pay.
The Congressman with a bad limp was bitter.
They had operated on the wrong leg, made it shorter.

My father's coal yards under a wartime heavy snow.
The big blue trucks wearing chains like S/M love.
Blessed are the poor, for they will have heat this Christmas.
The tire chains/sleigh bells go *chink chink*.

The crow at the foot of the bed caws you
Were the Age of Chivalry and gave my family coal.
And when it was hot your ice trucks delivered
To the colored their block of cold.

XXXII

HAMLET

The horsefly landing fatly on the page
And walking through words from left to right is rage.
It walks, stage right to left, across the stage.
The play is called *The Nest Becomes a Cage.*

I'm reading *Hamlet*, in which a bulging horsefly
Soliloquizes constantly, played by
Me. He's getting old, don't ask me why.
His lines are not familiar. Then I die.

I have been thinking, instead of weeping, tears,
And drinking everybody else's, for years.
They taste amazingly like urine. Cheers!
I tell you this—(But soft! My mother nears.)

You wonder how I know what urine tastes like?
I stuck my finger in a hole in a dike
And made the heart near-bursting burst. Strike
While it's hot. You have to seize the mike

And scream, "This is I! Hamlet the Dane!" True—
Too true—the lascivious iceberg you
Are cruising to, *Titanic*, is a Jew
Ophelia loved, a man she thought she knew.

One day I was bombing Belgrade, bombing Belgrade,
To halt the slaughter elsewhere, knowing aid
Arrives through the air in the form of a tirade
Hamlet stabs through the arras, like a man does a maid,

Only in this case it was the father of the girl,
Poor Polonius, her father. She is a pearl
At the bottom of a stream, and every curl
Of nothing but herself is drowned. I whirl

Around, and this is I! a fellow fanned
Into a flame. The horsefly that I land
On her has little legs—but on command
Struts back and forth on stage, princely, grand.

There are other examples but
A perfect example in his poetry is the what
Will save you factor.
The Jaws of Life cut the life crushed in the compactor

Out.
My life is a snout
Snuffling toward the truffle, life. Anyway!
It is a life of luxury. Don't put me out of my misery.

I am seeking more Jerusalem, not less.
And in the outtakes, after they pull my fingernails out, I confess:
I do love
The sky above.

FREDERICK SEIDEL

I live a life of laziness and luxury,
Like a hare without a bone who sleeps in a pâté.
I met a fellow who was so depressed
He never got dressed and never got undressed.

He lived a life of laziness and luxury.
He hid his life away in poetry,
Like a hare still running from a gun in a pâté.
He didn't talk much about himself because there wasn't much to

He found it was impossible to look or not to.
It will literally blind him but he's got to.
Her caterpillar with a groove
Waits for love

Between her legs. The crease
Is dripping grease.
He's blind—now he really is.
Can't you help him, gods!

Her light is white
Moonlight.
Or the Parthenon under the sun
Is the other one.